Tell, The World It's A Boy
By Jeanmela Murray

Tell The World It's A Boy.
1st Edition Copyright © May 2015
By Jeanmela Murray

A Cupcake & Giggles Publishing

This title is Also brought to you by: C.A.R.E Imprint (Children Are Reading Everyday)

All rights reserved. No part of this publication may be reproduced, distributed, or transmitted in any form or by any means, including photocopying, recording, or other electronic or mechanical methods, without the prior written permission of the publisher, except in the case of brief quotations embodied in critical reviews and certain other non-commercial uses permitted by copyright law. For permission requests, write to the publisher, addressed "Attention: Permissions Coordinator," at the email address below.

WWW.ICARE.IMPRINT@GMAIL.COM

Visit us: WWW.ACUPCAKEANDGIGGLESPUBLISHING.COM

Like Us: WWW.FACEBOOK.COM/TELLTHEWORLDCHILDRENSBOOKSERIES

TELL THE WORLD IT'S A GIRL IS ALSO AVAILABLE FROM THIS AUTHOR

Ordering Information: Tell the world book series are available at: acupcakeandgigglespublishing.com, amazon.com, specialty bookstores and online boutiques.

Please Contact a cupcake and giggles publishing for more details.
Quantity sales. Special discounts are available on quantity purchases by corporations, associations, and others. For details, contact the publisher at the email address above.

Published, Printed and Distributed in the United States of America

Printed and Distributed in Charleston, SC
ISBN-13: 978-0996384711
ISBN-10: 0996384715
BISAC: Juvenile Nonfiction / Family / New Baby
1st Edition Paperback May 2015
Book Design/Illustration by Jeanmela Murray

☻Tell The World It's A Boy☻

To LOVE: Out of the darkest night the sun did rise and gave me the most incredible prize! A gift, a treasure... A Daughter!! I waited for you all my life! With you, I'm filled with all I need. You are my greatest inspiration; I get to see a brand new world through your eyes and it's refreshingly beautiful. Thank you for choosing me! Let us forever go to the moon tonight my sweet precious baby girl! I love you beyond the skies, with no end...My Cupcake, My Orchid, My Lotus Flower, My Gamble, My Sunshine, My Rebel Heart, My Little Miss Sassy, My Life, My Zoee Catelaya...

GO BE BRILLIANT!!

Love Always,
Mommy (Your endless supply of love) ∞

◇◇◇

To My Amazing Family, Friends, and Supporters
THANK YOU, THANK YOU, THANKYOU ☺ XOXO

◇◇◇

Sons all over the world...OWN YOUR GREATNESS- Be Exceptional...No-one can put the color in your Dream but YOU!! Special Mention: LaFayette, Jordon, Calkin (Cam Cam), Jeffrey, Julius, Sevon, Jordon, Jace, Hunter, Haidir, Charles (CJ), Josiah, Josh

◇◇◇

My Parents: Melvin Leathers & Mamie Cora Jean WITHOUT YOU, THERE IS NO ME or ZOEE... I LOVE YOU!!! ∞

◇◇◇

My Angels-Aunt Judi <My Rainbow>: Epitome of Sass, Fierceness, Beauty, and Strength
Aunt Dot: Love, Grace, & Nurturer
My Sister Joy: Taken so soon but your light will continually shine through your niece and myself ∞Love U

● Tell The World It's A Boy ●

An Inscription to my Son

BOOK COVER SCAVENGER HUNT

1. Tell The World It's a Boy (2)
2. Bright Star... You have everything you need
3. Lucky Clover...Mom/Dad were blessed the day you were born
4. HEARTS (3)...Follow it & live without regret
5. BE BRILLIANT
6. Color splashes: Red, Yellow, Purple, Green, Blue (Paint the world your way)
7. Kiss... Especially when you need it most
8. SQUARE...."It's okay to be SQUARE, It's a gift ☺"
9. Black circles with diamonds...Keep tunnel vision to your DREAMS... Just like YOU, THEY ARE BEAUTIFUL
10. BRAVE, LEADER, BOY (You were born to lead)
11. I AM WHAT I THINK I AM (Your Words have Power...Use them wisely)
12. Hear Only that which supports your dreams
13. Be Unapologetically You (You Are Enough)
14. Color outside the lines (When you were born, you broke the mold. Don't Stop Now ...Do it your own way!!
15. LIVE, LIVE, LIVE (Life goes fast...Don't be just spectator in life)
16. It's okay not to be perfect but it's not okay to stop moving forward...KEEP MOVING
17. Strength...(Keep moving even when it doesn't come easy or it hurts)
18. Courage...(Be your most brilliant self without compromise)
19. Puzzle Piece (You hold the key to your life)
20. Foot Print...(Make Your Mark)
21. Flowers growing outside your mind(Your thoughts, dreams, and desires are Beautiful...You reap what you sow)
22. LOVE (Remember YOU are Worthy!)
23. CROWN & **5** Crown Jewels (Wear it proudly!)

☺Tell The World It's A Boy☺

I AM UNSTOPPABLE

_____
NAME

_____
FROM
ISBN-10:0996384715
ISBN-13:978-0-9963847-1-1

● Tell The World It's A Boy ●

It's a Boy, a **Handsome** little Boy; an Angel you are and we are happily in

love with you....

Beautiful eyes, nose, and lips

Oh my precious son, before you, the world seemed like a total eclipse ....

  SAD

H*A*PPY

☺Tell The World It's A Boy☺

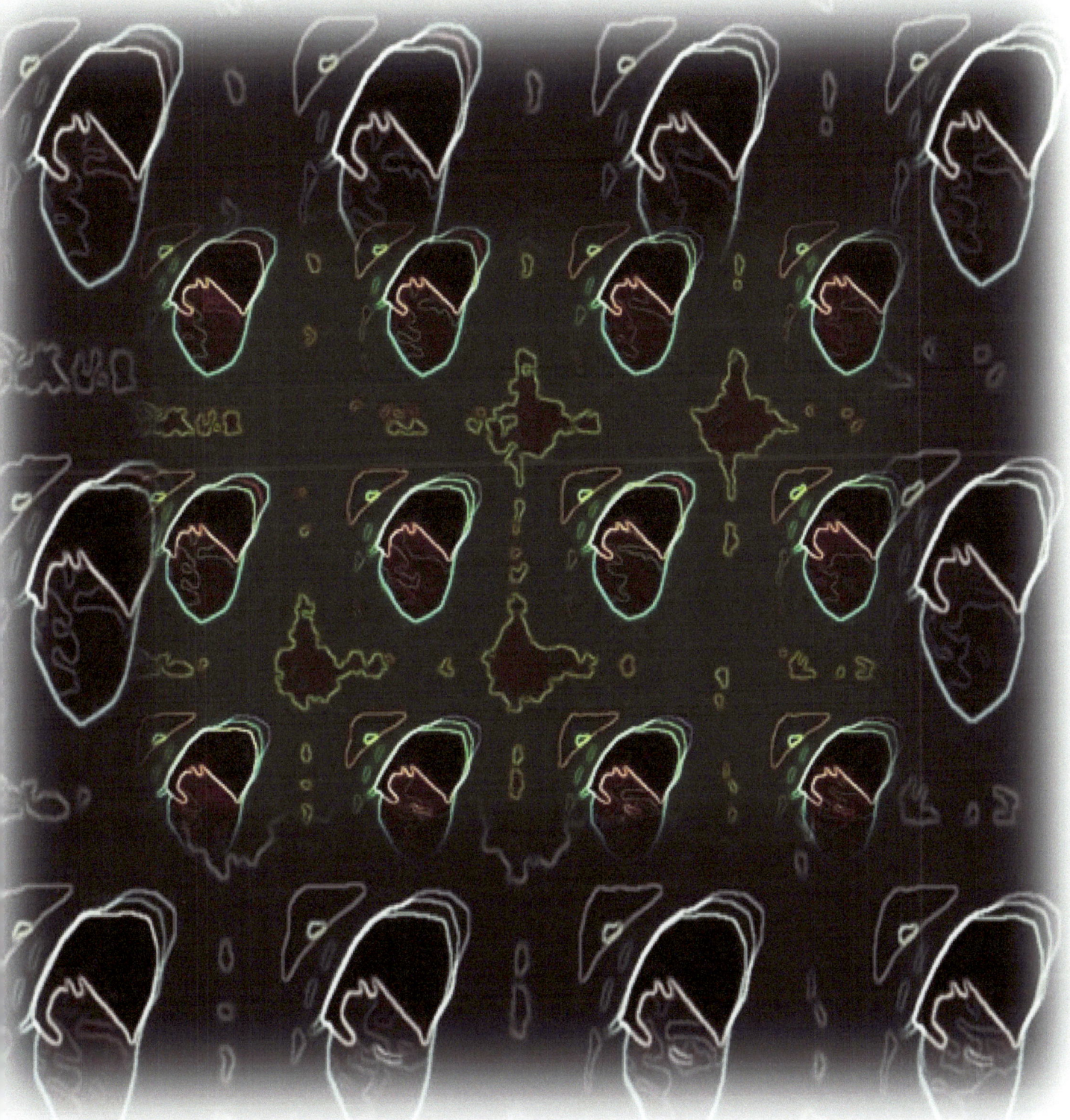

It's a Boy, a **Mesmerizing** little Boy; what an Angel you are!

A dream come true the first time we laid eyes on you....

You're Perfect in every way! Hair filled with magical curlicues, skin so soft,

scent so sweet, and totally kissable little feet....

☺Tell The World It's A Boy☺

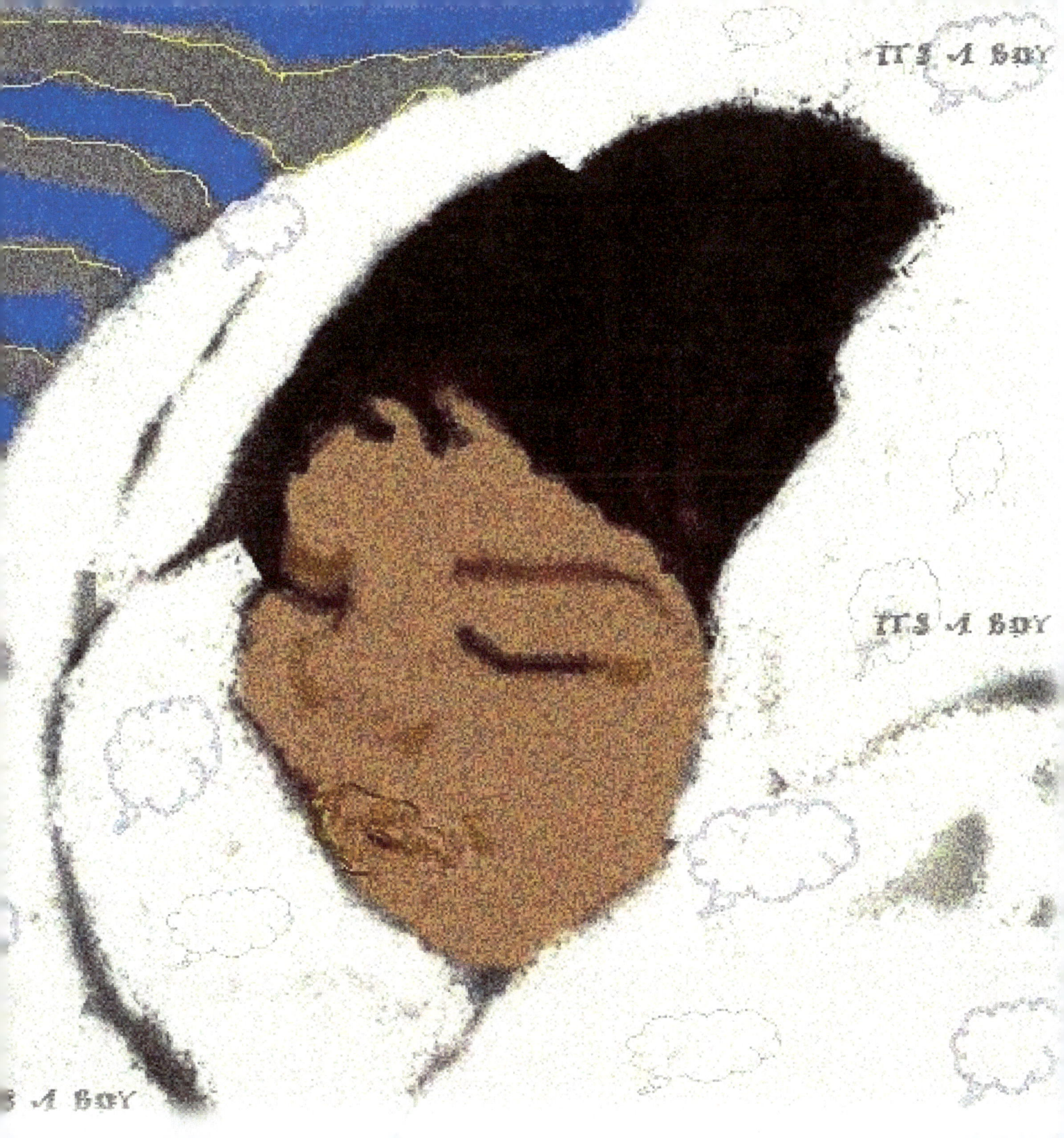

It's a Boy, a Heaven-Sent little Boy; what an Angel you are!

Time stood still the moment you were born....

The world is oh so busy and for the rest of our lives no nap or sleep for We,

but there is no place on Earth we'd rather be....

It's a Boy, a Spirited little Boy; what an Angel you are!

Thank you for choosing us; in our hearts is where you will always be....

Blushing little jowls and giggly giggles, but Mommy and Daddy can't help it; you're as charming as charming can be....

You'll forever feel the fullness of our hearts;

They flutter through the sky as kisses and land on your cheek

•THANK HEAVEN FOR LITTLE BOYS•

It's a Boy, a Delightful little Boy; what an Angel you are! The cure for sad faces and broken hearts, morning, noon, and night....

One look at you and this unyielding world seems new....

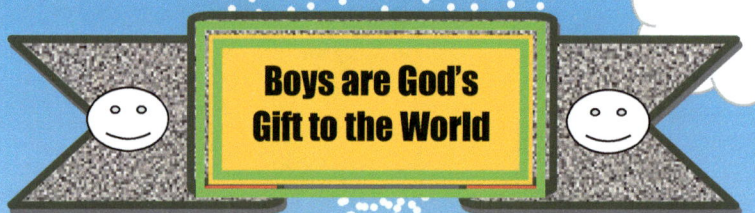

Boys are God's Gift to the World

It's a Boy, a **Majestic** little Boy; what an Angel you are! Whether near or far, from 𝓐 to 𝓩 you will always be mommy and daddy's brightest star....

Eyes twinkle brighter than the constellations and a smile as divine as a full moon; we get lost in your joyfulness and splendor like a Sunday afternoon....

◎Tell The World It's A Boy◎

● Tell The World It's A Boy ●

It's a Boy, a **Dapper** little Boy; what an Angel you are! Bright eyes and picturesque smile, you're going places for sure;

Already displaying instant wit and guile....

You can be a genius in anything you choose. Math, science, language, history, business, or art;

It doesn't matter as long as you have passion and heart!

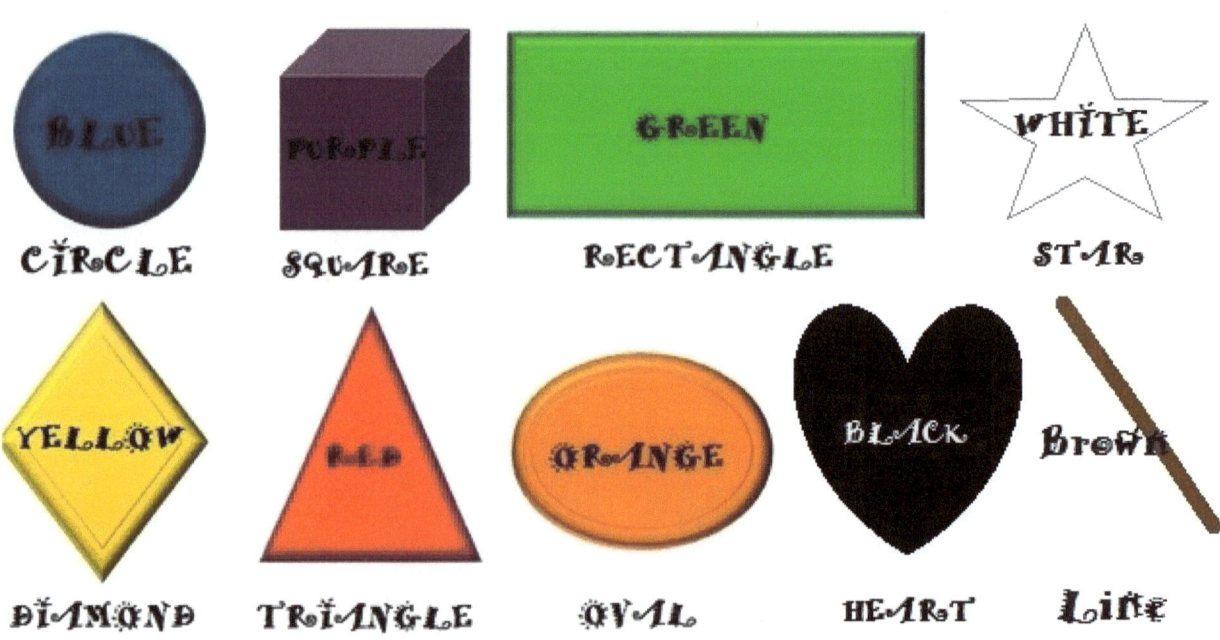

☻Tell The World It's A Boy☻

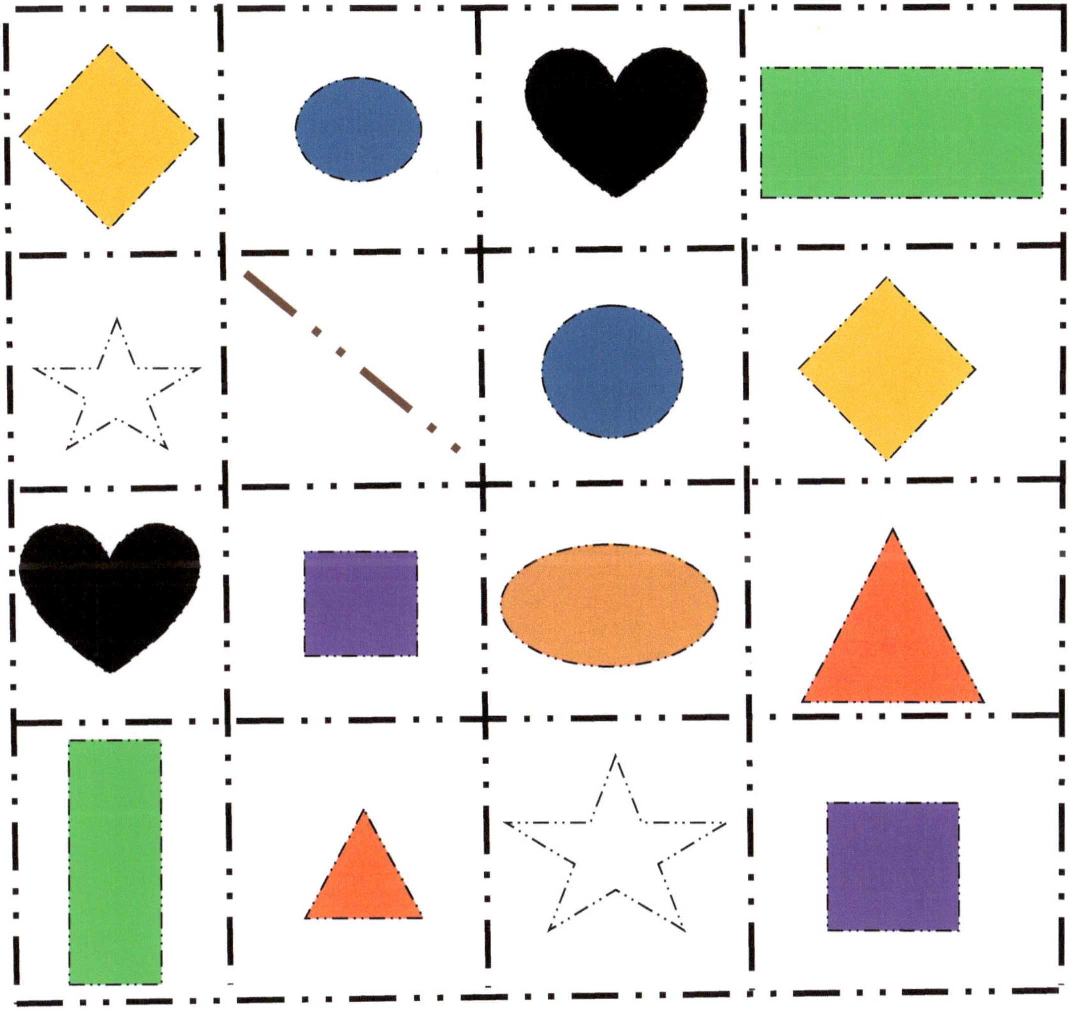

The world is painted with shapes... Shape your world or someone else will!
#ICHOOSE

● Tell The World It's A Boy ●

It's a Boy,

An Impressionable little Boy;

What an Angel you are!

Mommy and daddy's pint-sized reflection,

Good role models are what we vow to be, as your little eyes look up to thee....

So pure and full of possibility,

We're so blessed and grateful to have this opportunity;

The chance to help you grow with

Love, life, hope, and liberty....

☻Tell The World It's A Boy☻

LOVE

LIFE

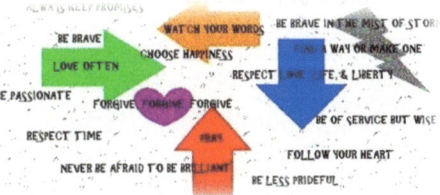

HOPE

● Tell The World It's A Boy ●

LIBERTY

It's a Boy, a Flourishing little Boy; what an Angel you are!

Small hands, small feet... Oh my, how time flies, you have two front teeth....

Just yesterday we were carrying you along and today you're walking,

running, and eating all on your own. Please don't grow up too fast, be a

child as long as you can, and we'll promise to hold your precious hand.

When it's time, not a minute or moment before,

You'll be able to hold your own for sure....

☺Tell The World It's A Boy☺

● Tell The World It's A Boy ●

It's a Boy, a Captivating little Boy; what an Angel you are!

So honey sweet, scrumptious and divine; God's best Heavenly surprise....

We are so honored to call you our son.

Life has truly just begun. From the rising of the Sun to the glorious Moon,

The Stars are singing a Heavenly tune.

Oh What a Blessing You Are....

It's a Boy,
A *Future Leader* little Boy; what an Angel you are!
Stand straight and tall our leading young man,
You were born with purpose and power....
Always do your best and accept nothing less.
Never dim your light to please others; you are better off being alone than amongst those who don't want the best for you. Use your mind and you can conquer anything. Your legs are sturdy and your heart is strong; your discerning spirit will help carry you along. Remember, you Lead by walking in your own truth. Utilize your heart for more than just beating; be passionate, wise, and prayerful. Son,
If you are authentically being yourself, there is
Nothing you cannot do; add a smile and there is
No way can you lose!

☺Tell The World It's A Boy☺

 MY MIND & TONGUE ARE MY MOST POWERFUL INSTRUMENTS ... I WILL USE THEM BOTH WISELY

1) STOP THINKING "I WISH"
2) START SAYING "I WILL"
3) NOW PROVE YOURSELF RIGHT BY DOING IT!

Be Brave, Bold, and Brilliant! Go on adventures inside and out of your mind, reach for the stars and climb, climb, climb. Be Unapologetically you! Play outside; build skyscrapers, rumble with fire flies, make mud pies, & color outside the lines <This is your life> You only get one!
So have fun, try lots of scary new things, and scour high in the trees; let your captivating locs dance in the breeze. Read new books, find exciting things to cook up, Fox Trot with hope, and write your own storybook. Tap dance in the clouds, sing amongst the birds, and live, live, live. Ambitiously Pursue 10,000 pound dreams and hunt camouflaged "no's" until you reach your pot of gold... Even if no one else believe, Trust in yourself* & follow your heart;* don't be afraid to capture your dreams* because just like you, they are Beautiful*

☻Tell The World It's A Boy☻

I AM prepared to get to MY YES

1 NO 2 NO 3 NO 4 NO 5 NO 6 NO 7 NO 8 NO 9 NO 10 YES

I WILL FIND A WAY OR MAKE ONE

I will patiently pursue my "Yes" with a loyal & optimistic attitude... I AM WORTH IT!

Trust in yourself* & follow your heart; don't be afraid to capture your dreams* because just like you, they are Beautiful*

It's a Boy, a **Handsome**, **Mesmerizing**, Heaven-Sent, **Spirited**, **Delightful**, **Majestic**, **Dapper**, Impressionable, **Flourishing**, **Captivating**, and a **Future Leader** little Boy. What an Extraordinary Son you are! A true treasure sent to Earth, We are happily in love with you! We will shout it out from mountains high to valleys low, tell the whole world; so this day, everyone will know about our greatest blessing named——! Say your name with us,——, it's a magical sound, Go on; speak it proudly and make it sing over the lands . Yes You Can, Yes You Can, and Yes You Will! So, my dearest little Prince, when you feel small in this big-big world, just listen for the birds singing, see fish swimming, the flowers blooming, and the animals dancing; they are all telling the world....

It's our Handsome little Boy, mommy and daddy's true life Angel, and

We are Happily in Love with YOU 💙

● Tell The World It's A Boy ●

About the Author

Jeanmela Murray was born and raised in Akron, Ohio. She is a graduate of American InterContinental University with a B.F.A in Fashion Merchandising and Fashion Design and later polished the city as a nail technician. Currently, Jeanmela resides in Atlanta, Georgia since 1999. In 2012 she became the mother of a beautiful little girl named Zoee, whom became the inspiration behind her wanting to write children's stories. What started out as a heart-felt message to her daughter, grew another love for wanting other children to feel the same type of love she saw in her daughter's eyes. Jeanmela wanted children to know they are beautiful and are God's gifts to the world. Zoee loves books and Jeanmela would love for other children to have that same excitement. She is in the process of developing a reading program called C.A.R.E (Children Are Reading Everyday) hoping to bring families together, morning, noon, and night. Through C.A.R.E, Jeanmela will allot her books to disadvantage families too facilitate stronger family bonds while they are going through tough times. She also would like other local authors to donate books to this cause. All parents deserve to see their children's face light up! I want to help families escape their challenging reality, even if only for a brief moment, says Jeanmela. She is optimistic her books will make a difference, getting families to read collectively and find comfort in the little things!

Additional Tidbits:

Jeanmela loves writing, music, photography, poetry, sports, designing jewelry, and nail polish!
A few of her most favorite moments are the birth of her baby girl, seeing her daughter smile & giggle while running through the water sprinklers, and waking up to her kisses. Other notable highlights for Jeanmela are designing jewelry for Singer/Song writer India.Arie and Laurnea Wilkerson, autographing books for her first poetry book release, and watching her favorite athlete, Serena Williams play tennis.

In the future, Jeanmela will continue spreading love and encourage children to become their most powerful selves through her literary works for children.
Also Available from Author Jeanmela Murray:

☺ Tell The World It's A Girl ☺

☺Tell The World It's A Boy☺

www.ingramcontent.com/pod-product-compliance
Lightning Source LLC
Chambersburg PA
CBHW060823090426
42738CB00002B/92